THE
GAME OF LIFE
AND
HOW TO PLAY IT

THE
GAME OF LIFE
AND
HOW TO PLAY IT

by
Florence Scovel Shinn

The Timeless Classic on Successful Living

Abridged and Introduced
by Mitch Horowitz

THE CONDENSED CLASSICS LIBRARY™

Published by Gildan Media LLC
aka G&D Media.
www.GandDmedia.com

The Game of Life and How to Play It was originally published in 1925
G&D Media Condensed Classics edition published 2018
Abridgement and Introduction copyright © 2015 by Mitch Horowitz

FIRST EDITION: 2018

Cover design by David Rheinhardt of Pyrographx

Interior design by Meghan Day Healey of Story Horse, LLC.

ISBN: 978-1-7225-0053-5

CONTENTS

Philosopher of Everyday Life

A sk any fan of motivational or New Thought literature to name his or her favorite books, and chances are the list will include Florence Scovel Shinn's *The Game of Life and How to Play It.*

Shinn's book has been beloved among self-help readers since it first appeared in 1925. Yet it almost didn't appear at all. Shinn, a respected illustrator of children's literature, could not get New York publishers interested in her metaphysical philosophy. Finding no takers, the artist published the book herself.

Shinn's outlook is simple and decisive. Within you, she writes, exist three minds: the *conscious mind*, which you use to navigate daily life; the *subconscious mind*, which acts on suggestions, good or bad, from your conscious mind; and the *superconscious mind,* a spark of divine power within you. Your superconscious, she writes, possesses infinite awareness and the creative ability to remake your world. Shinn provides methods to get in tune with this higher mind, and thus "win" at the game of life.

What accounts for Shinn's longstanding popularity? Her ideas were not unique to her time. Contemporaneous metaphysical writers, such as William Walker Atkinson and Wallace D. Wattles, held similar views. Yet listening to Shinn always feels like hearing from a trusted friend—someone who understands our daily struggles and who doesn't talk above us; but who also isn't afraid to deliver tough advice and won't tolerate excuses. She insists that we get out there and test her methods on the field of life.

Shinn was a lasting influence on many leaders in the positive-thinking movement, including Emmett Fox, Norman Vincent Peale, and Louise Hay. It is notable that each of these figures is from a different generation: Fox, a popular New Thought minister, was a contemporary of Shinn's; Peale, a Methodist minister, rose to worldwide fame in the 1950s as the author of *The Power of Positive Thinking*; and Hay is widely known today as a pioneering New Age publisher and writer. Martin Luther King's eldest daughter, Yolanda, told me shortly before her death in 2007 that Shinn's writing had influenced her. This gives some sense of Shinn's range of impact.

While Shinn called life a "game," her own life was not easy—nor did she seek ease. Born Florence Scovel in Camden, New Jersey in 1871, she took a rare path as a female artist, attending the Pennsylvania Academy of Fine Arts. There she met her future husband, realist painter Everett Shinn. Married in 1898, they moved to New York's Greenwich Village, where they became part of the Ashcan School of American artists, a cohort known for depicting street scenes, tenements, and the immigrant experience. The couple divorced in 1912. While pursuing her own career as an illustrator, Shinn became a student of metaphysics, leading her to write *The Game of Life* and several other books. She also became a popular spiritual lecturer and counselor. She died in Manhattan in 1940.

One of the defining elements of Shinn's work is its bravery. Shinn neither sought, nor received, mainstream approval. Instead, she embodied a core ideal of American metaphysics: that the common person, the everyday man or woman, is as capable of receiving higher truths as the Biblical prophets of antiquity. Nearly a century after her first book, Shinn has proven the endurance of her message.

—Mitch Horowitz

CHAPTER ONE

The Game

Most people consider life a battle, but it is not a battle, it is a game.

It is a game, however, that cannot be played successfully without knowledge of spiritual law, and the Old and New Testaments give the rules of the game with wonderful clarity. Jesus Christ taught that life is a great game of *Giving* and *Receiving*.

"Whatsoever a man soweth that shall he also reap." This means that whatever a person sends out in word or deed, will return to him; what he gives, he will receive— hate for hate; love for love; criticism for criticism.

We are also taught that the imaging faculty of the mind plays a leading part in the game of life. "Keep thy heart (or imagination) with all diligence, for out of it are the issues of life." (Proverbs 4:23) This means that what you image in your mind, sooner or later, externalizes in your life.

To successfully play the game of life you must train the imaging faculty. A person with an imaging faculty disciplined to image only good brings into his life "every righteous desire of his heart"—health, wealth, love, friends, perfect self-expression, and high ideals.

To train the imagination successfully, you must understand the workings of your mind. It has three departments: the *subconscious, conscious*, and *superconscious*. The subconscious is simply power without direction. It is like steam or electricity, and it does what it is directed to do. Whatever you feel deeply or image clearly is impressed upon your subconscious, and carried out in minutest detail.

The conscious mind has been called mortal or carnal mind. It is your ordinary human mind, and it sees life as it *appears to be.* It sees death, disaster, sickness, poverty, and limitation of every kind, which it impresses on your subconscious.

The *superconscious* mind is the God Mind within us all, and is the realm of perfect ideas. In it is the "perfect pattern" spoken of by Plato, *The Divine Design*—for there is a *Divine Design* for each one of us.

There is a place that you are to fill and no one else can fill, something you are to do, that no one else can do.

A perfect picture of this divine plan exists in your *superconscious mind*. It usually flashes across your conscious mind as an unattainable ideal—"something too good to be true." In reality, this is your true destiny (or destination) coming to you from Infinite Intelligence, which is *within you*.

Many people are ignorant of their true destinies. They strive for things and situations that do not belong to them, and would bring only failure and dissatisfaction if attained.

For example, a woman asked me to "speak the word" that she would marry a certain man. (She called him A.B.) I replied that this would be a violation of spiritual law, but that I would speak the word for the *right man*, the "divine selection."

I added, "If A.B. is the right man you can't lose him; and if he isn't, you will receive his equivalent." She saw A.B. frequently but made no headway in their friendship. One evening she said, "You know, for the last week A.B. hasn't seemed so wonderful to me." I replied, "Maybe he is not the divine selection—another man may be the right one."

Soon after, she did meet another man, who fell in love with her at once and who told her she was his ideal. In fact, he said all the things that she had always wished A.B. would say to her.

This illustration shows the law of substitution. A right idea was substituted for a wrong one and, hence, no loss or sacrifice was entailed. Jesus said, "Seek ye first the Kingdom of God and his righteousness; and all these things shall be added unto you," and he said the Kingdom is *within man*.

The Kingdom is the realm of *right ideas*, or the divine pattern, revealed to us by our superconscious mind, or Christ within. In the following chapters we will learn more about the awesome possibilities of this power within us.

CHAPTER TWO

The Law of Prosperity

One of the greatest messages given to humanity through Scripture is that God is man's supply, and that man can release, *through his spoken word*, all that is his by divine right. He must, however, have *perfect faith in his spoken word*.

Isaiah said, "My word shall not return unto me void, but shall accomplish that where unto it is sent." Words and thoughts are a tremendous vibratory force, ever molding man's body and affairs.

But remember, if one asks for success and prepares for failure, he will get the situation he has prepared for. A man once asked me to speak the word that a certain debt would be wiped out. I found that he spent his time planning what he would say to his debtor when he did not pay his bill, thereby neutralizing my words. He should have seen himself paying the debt.

We see a wonderful depiction of this in the Bible, relating to three kings in the desert, who were without water for their men and horses. They consulted the prophet Elisha, who gave them this astonishing message: "Thus saith the Lord—Ye shall not see wind, neither shall ye see rain, yet make this valley full of ditches."

You must prepare for the thing you have asked for *when there isn't the slightest sign of it.*

Your adverse thoughts, doubt, and fear surge from the subconscious. They are the "army of the aliens," which must be put to flight. Having made a statement of high spiritual truth, you have challenged the old beliefs in your subconscious, and "error is exposed" to be put out. In fact, a big demonstration is usually preceded by tormenting thoughts. This explains why it is often "darkest before the dawn."

At these times of challenge, you must make your affirmations of truth repeatedly, and rejoice and give thanks that you have already received. "Before ye call I shall answer." This means that "every good and perfect gift" is already yours, awaiting your recognition.

The children of Israel were told that they could have all the land they could see. This is true for each of us. You have only the land within your own mental vision. Every great work, every big accomplishment, has been brought into manifestation through holding to the vision, and often just before the big achievement, comes apparent failure and discouragement.

When the children of Israel reached the "Promised Land" they were afraid to enter, for they said it was filled with giants who made they feel like grasshoppers. This is almost everyone's experience. The one who knows spiritual law, however, is undisturbed by appearance, and rejoices while he is "yet in captivity." He holds to his vision, and gives thanks that the end is accomplished.

CHAPTER THREE

The Power of the Word

A person who knows *the power of the word* becomes very careful of his conversation. He has only to watch the reaction of his words to know that they do "not return void." Through his spoken word man is continually making laws for himself.

I have a friend who often says on the phone, "Do come to see me and have a fine old-fashioned chat." This "old-fashioned chat" means an hour of about five hundred to a thousand destructive words, the principal topics being loss, lack, failure, and sickness.

I reply: "No, thank you, I've had enough old-fashioned chats in my life; they are too expensive. But I will be glad to have a new-fashioned chat, and talk about what we want, not what we don't want."

There is an old saying that man only dares use his words for three purposes: to "heal, bless, or prosper."

What you say of others will be said of you, and what you wish for another, you are wishing for yourself.

Your only true enemies are within. The enlightened person, therefore, endeavors to perfect himself on his neighbor. His work is to send out goodwill and blessings to every being. And the marvelous thing is, if you bless a man he has no power to harm you. *Goodwill produces a great aura of protection about the one who sends it, and "No weapon that is formed against him shall prosper." In other words, love and goodwill destroy the enemies within one's self—therefore, one has no enemies on the external.*

There is peace on earth for him who sends goodwill to man.

CHAPTER FOUR

The Law of Nonresistance

Nothing on earth can resist an absolutely non-resistant person.

The Chinese say that water is the most powerful element because it is perfectly nonresistant. It can wear away a rock, and sweep all that is before it.

Jesus said, "Resist not evil," for He knew, in reality, there is no evil, therefore nothing to resist. Evil has come of man's "vain imagination," or a belief in two powers: good and evil.

There is an old legend that Adam and Eve ate of "Maya the Tree of Illusion," and saw two powers instead of one power, God. *Therefore, evil is a false law that man has made for himself.*

Man's soul is his subconscious mind, and whatever he feels deeply, good or bad, is outpictured by that faithful servant. His body and affairs reflect what he has been picturing. The sick man has pictured his sickness, the poor man, poverty, the rich man, wealth. Children are sensitive and receptive to the thoughts of others about them, and often outpicture the fears of their parents.

A metaphysician once said, "If you do not run your subconscious mind yourself, someone else will run it for you." The man who is centered and established in right thinking, the man who sends out only goodwill, and who is without fear, cannot be *touched or influenced by the negative thoughts of others.*

Some of us are kept in bondage by thoughts of the past. Living in the past is a failure and a violation of spiritual law. The past keeps you blocked. You must bless it and forget it; you should likewise bless the future, knowing that it has in store for you endless joys; but you must live *fully in the now.*

Make this affirmation immediately upon waking: *Thy will be done this day! Today is a day of completion; I give thanks for this perfect day, miracle shall follow miracle, and wonders shall never cease.*

Make this a daily habit—and you *will* see wonders and miracles enter your life.

Chapter Five

The Law of Karma

The Game of Life is a game of boomerangs. Man's thoughts, deeds, and words return to him, sooner or later, with astounding accuracy.

This is the Law of Karma, which is another way of saying, "Whatsoever a man soweth, that also shall he reap."

The more you know about the Game of Life, the more you are responsible for. Someone with knowledge of Spiritual Law who does not practice it, suffers greatly in consequence. In the Bible, if we read the word Lord as law it will make many passages much clearer. "The fear of the Lord (law) is the beginning of wisdom."

Always remember that *your desires are a tremendous force; they must be directed in the right channels or chaos ensues.*

In demonstrating, the first and most important step is to *ask aright*. Man should always demand only that which is his by *divine right*. We are admonished: "My will be done not thine." And man always gets just what he desires when he *relinquishes personal will*, thereby enabling Infinite Intelligence to work through him. "Stand ye still and see the salvation of the Lord (law)."

A woman came to me in great distress. Her daughter had determined to take a very hazardous trip, and the mother was filled with fear. She had used every argument, had pointed out the dangers, and forbidden her to go. But the daughter became only more rebellious and determined. I told the mother, "You are forcing your personal will upon your daughter, which you have no right to do. Your fear of the trip is only attracting it, for we attract what we fear."

I added, "Let go, and take your mental hands off. *Put it in God's hands, and use this statement*: 'I put this situation in the hands of Infinite Love and Wisdom; if this trip is the Divine plan, I bless it and no longer resist; but if it is not divinely planned, I give thanks that it is now dissolved and dissipated.'"

A day or so later, her daughter told her, "Mother I have given up the trip," and the situation returned to its "native nothingness."

Sometimes our most difficult challenge is that of "standing still." But when we can do that, and turn life over to the Divine Will, events have their perfect outcome.

CHAPTER SIX

Casting the Burden
(Impressing the Subconscious)

When you understand the workings of your mind, your great desire is to find an easy and quick way to impress the subconscious with good; for simply an intellectual knowledge of Truth will not bring results.

I have found that the easiest way is in "casting the burden."

In the fifty-fifth Psalm we are told to "cast thy burden upon the Lord." Many passages in the Bible state that the *battle is God's* not man's, and that man is always to *"stand still"* and *see the Salvation of the Lord*.

That is what Jesus meant when he said, "My yoke is easy and my burden is light." He further said: "Come to me all ye that labor and are heavy laden, and I will give you rest."

This indicates that the superconscious mind (or Christ within) is the department that fights man's battle and relieves him of burdens. We see, therefore, that man violates the law if he carries a burden. And a burden is an adverse thought or condition, and this thought or condition has its root in the subconscious.

It seems almost impossible to make any headway directing the subconscious from the conscious, or reasoning, mind, as the reasoning mind (the intellect) is limited in its conceptions and filled with doubts and fears.

How scientific it then is to cast the burden upon the superconscious mind (or Christ within) where it is "made light," or dissolved into its "native nothingness."

A woman in urgent need of money "made light" upon the Christ within, the superconscious, with this statement: "I cast this burden of lack on the Christ within and I go free to have plenty." The belief in lack was her burden, and as she cast it upon the superconscious, with its belief in plenty, an avalanche of supply resulted.

I knew a woman whose burden was resentment. For years, resentment held her in a state of torment and imprisoned her soul (the subconscious mind). She said: "I cast this resentment on the Christ within and I go free to be loving, harmonious, and happy." The Almighty superconscious flooded the subconscious, and her whole life was changed.

When you "cast the burden," your statement should be made over and over and over, sometimes for hours at a time, silently or audibly, with quietness but determination.

I have noticed in "casting the burden" that after a little while one seems to see clearly. It is impossible to have clear vision while in the throes of the carnal mind. In steadily repeating the affirmation, "I cast this burden on the Christ within and go free," the vision clears, and with it comes a feeling of relief and, sooner or later, *the manifestation of good*.

A student once asked me to explain the "darkness before the dawn." As noted earlier, often before a big demonstration "everything seems to go wrong," and deep depression clouds the consciousness. This means that out of the subconscious are rising doubts and fears of the ages. These old derelicts of the subconscious rise to the surface *to be put out*. It is just then that a man should clap his symbols, like Jehoshaphat, and give thanks that he is saved, even though he seems surrounded by the enemy.

The student continued, "How long must one remain in the dark?" I replied, "Until one *can see in the dark*," and *"Casting the burden enables one to see in the dark."*

In order to impress the subconscious, active faith is essential. Jesus showed active faith when "He commanded the multitude to sit down on the ground," before He gave thanks for the loaves and fishes.

Active faith is the bridge over which man passes to the Promised Land. I will give another example showing how necessary this step is.

A woman I knew had, through misunderstanding, been separated from her husband, whom she loved deeply. He refused all offers of reconciliation. Coming into knowledge of Spiritual Law, she denied the appearance of separation. She made this statement: "There is no separation in Divine Mind, therefore, I cannot be separated from the love and companionship which are mine by divine right."

She showed active faith by arranging a place for him at the table every day, thereby impressing the subconscious with a picture of his return. More than a year passed, but she never wavered, and *one day he walked in.*

The student must remember not to despise the "day of small things." Invariably, before a demonstration come "signs of land." Before Columbus reached America, he saw birds and twigs, which showed him land was near. So it is with a demonstration; but often the student mistakes it for the demonstration itself, and is disappointed.

For example, a woman had "spoken the word" for a set of dishes. Not long afterwards a friend gave her a dish that was old and cracked. She came to me and said, "Well, I asked for a set of dishes, and all I got was a cracked plate."

I replied, "The plate was only 'signs of land.' It shows your dishes are coming—look upon it as birds and twigs." And not long afterward the dishes came.

CHAPTER SEVEN

Love

A woman came to me in deep distress. The man she loved had left her for another women, and said he had never intended to marry her. She was torn with jealousy and resentment, and said she hoped he would suffer as he had made her suffer. She added, "How could he leave me when I loved him so much?"

I replied, "You are not loving that man, you are hating him," and added, "*You can never receive what you have never given. Give a perfect love and you will receive a perfect love.* Perfect yourself on this man. Give him *unselfish* love, demanding nothing in return; do not criticize or condemn, and *bless him wherever he is.*"

I continued, "When you *send out real love*, real love will return to you. Either from this man or his equivalent, for if this man is not the divine selection you will not want him. As you are one with God, you are one with the love that is yours by divine right."

I told her of a brotherhood in India who never said, "Good morning" to each other. They used the words: *"I salute the Divinity in you."* They saluted the divinity in every man, for they *saw only God in every living thing.*

I said, "Salute the divinity in this man, and say, 'I see your divine self only. I see you as God sees you: perfect, made in His image and likeness.'"

She did so—and gradually she grew more poised and began losing her resentment. One morning I received a letter saying, "We are married."

There is an old proverb, "No man is your enemy, no man is your friend, every man is your teacher." This woman's lover was teaching her selfless love.

Suffering is not necessary for man's development; it is the result of violation of spiritual law, but few seem able to rouse themselves from their "soul sleep" without it. When people are happy, they usually become selfish, and automatically the Law of Karma is set in action. Man often suffers loss through lack of appreciation.

No one can attract money, for example, if he despises it. Many people are kept in poverty by saying "money means nothing to me." This is why so many artists are poor. Their contempt for money separates them from it. I remember hearing one artist say of another, "He's no good as an artist; he has money in the bank." This attitude of mind separates man from his supply; you must be in harmony with a thing in order to attract it.

Follow the path of love, and all things are added. For *God is love*—and *God is supply*.

Chapter Eight

Intuition or Guidance

No accomplishment is too great for the man who knows the power of his word, and who follows his intuitive leads. By the word he sets in action unseen forces, and can rebuild his body or remold his affairs.

It is, therefore, of utmost importance that the student choose the *right words,* and carefully select the affirmation he wishes to catapult into the invisible. He knows that God is his supply, that there is a supply for every demand, and that his spoken word releases this supply. "Ask and ye shall receive."

But it falls to man to make the first move. "Draw nigh to God and He will draw nigh to you."

I am often asked just how to make a demonstration. I reply, "Speak the word and then do nothing until you get a definite lead." Demand the lead, saying, "Infinite Spirit, reveal to me the way, let me know if there is anything for me to do."

The answer will come through intuition (or hunch); a chance remark from someone, or a passage in a book, etc. Intuition is a spiritual faculty and does not explain but simply *points the way*. The answers coming from intuition are sometimes startling in their exactness.

For example, a woman desired a large sum of money. She spoke the words: "Infinite Spirit, open the way for my immediate supply, let all that is mine by divine right now reach me, in great avalanches of abundance." Then she added: "Give me a definite lead, let me know if there is anything for me to do."

The thought came quickly, "Give a certain friend" (who had helped her spiritually) "a hundred dollars." She told her friend, who said, "Wait and get another lead before giving it." So she waited, and that day met a woman who said to her, "I gave someone a dollar today; it was just as much for me as it would be for you to give someone a hundred." This was an unmistakable lead, so she knew she was right in giving the hundred dollars. It was a gift that proved a great investment, for shortly after, a large sum of money came to her in a remarkable way.

Giving opens the way for receiving. In order to create activity in finances, one should give. Tithing, or giving one-tenth of one's income, is an old Jewish custom, and is sure to bring increase. The tenth-part goes forth and returns blessed and multiplied. But the gift or tithe must be given with love and cheerfulness, for "God loveth a cheerful giver." Bills should be paid cheerfully; all money should be sent forth happily and with a blessing.

This attitude of mind makes you a master of money. It obeys you, and your spoken word opens vast reservoirs of wealth.

CHAPTER NINE

Perfect Self-Expression
or the Divine Design

There is for each of us perfect self-expression. *There is a place for you to fill that no one else can fill; something you are to do that no one else can do; it is your destiny.*

Your personal achievement is held as a perfect idea in Divine Mind awaiting your recognition. As the imaging faculty is the creative faculty, it is necessary for you to see the idea before it can manifest.

So, your highest demand is for the *Divine Design of your life.*

You may not have the faintest conception of what it is. There is, possibly, some marvelous talent hidden deep within you.

Your demand should be: *"Infinite Spirit, open the way for the Divine Design of my life to manifest; let the genius within me now be released; let me see clearly the perfect plan."*

Your plan includes health, wealth, love, and perfect self-expression. This is the *square of life*, which brings perfect happiness. When you have made this demand, you may find great changes occurring in your life, for nearly everyone has wandered far from the Divine Design.

Many a genius has struggled for years with the problem of supply, when his spoken word, and faith, would have quickly released the necessary funds. After class one day a man came to me and handed me a cent. He said: "I have just seven cents in the world, and I'm going to give you one; for I have faith in the power of your spoken word. I want you to speak the word for my perfect self-expression and prosperity."

I "spoke the word," and did not see him again until a year later. He came in one day, successful and happy, with a roll of bills in his pocket. He said, "Immediately after you spoke the word, I had a position offered me in a distant city, and am now demonstrating health, happiness, and supply."

Demand definite leads for yourself, and the way will be made easy and successful.

One should not visualize or force a mental picture. When you demand the Divine Design to come into your conscious mind, you will receive flashes of inspiration and begin to see yourself making some great accomplishment. This is the picture, or idea, you must hold without wavering.

The thing you seek is seeking you—*the telephone was seeking Alexander Graham Bell.*

Now, one sure way of blocking your Divine Plan is *anger.* Anger blurs the visions, poisons the blood, is the root of many diseases, and causes wrong decision. It has been called one of the worst "sins" as its reaction is so harmful. The student learns that in metaphysics sin has a much broader meaning than in the old teaching. "Whatsoever is not of faith is of sin."

Fear and worry are deadly sins. They are inverted faith, and through distorted mental pictures, bring to pass the thing one fears. Your work is to drive out these enemies (from the subconscious mind).

You can vanquish fear only by walking up to the thing you are afraid of. When Jehoshaphat and his army prepared to meet the enemy singing, "Praise the Lord, for his mercy endureth forever" they found their enemies had destroyed each other—and there was nothing to fight.

CHAPTER TEN

Denials and Affirmations

A ll the good that is to be made manifest in your life is already an accomplished fact in the Divine Mind, and is released through your recognition, or spoken word. So you must be careful to decree that only the Divine Idea be made manifest; for often we decree through our "idle words," bringing failure and misfortune.

Again, it is of the utmost importance to word your demands correctly.

If you a desire home, friend, position, or any other good thing, make the demand for the "divine selection." For example, say: "Infinite Spirit, open the way for my right home, my right friend, my right position. I give thanks *that it now manifests under grace in a perfect way.*"

As you grow in financial consciousness, you should demand that the enormous sums of money, which are yours by divine right, reach you under grace in perfect ways.

It is impossible for you to release more than you think is possible, for you are bound by the limited expectancies of the subconscious. You must enlarge your expectancies in order to receive in a larger way.

The French illustrate this in a legend. A poor man was walking along a road when he met a traveler, who stopped him and said: "My good friend, I see you are poor. Take this gold nugget, sell it, and you will be rich all your days."

The man was overjoyed at his good fortune, and took the nugget home. He immediately found work and became so prosperous that he did not sell the nugget. Years passed, and he became very rich. One day he met a poor man on the road. He stopped him and said: "My good friend, I will give you this gold nugget, which, if you sell it, will make you rich for life." The mendicant took the nugget, had it valued, and found it was only brass. So, we see, the first man became rich through feeling rich, thinking the nugget was gold.

Feeling that a thing is so establishes it in the subconscious. It would not be necessary to make an affirmation more than once if one had perfect faith. One should not plead or supplicate, but give thanks repeatedly that he has received.

The Lord's Prayer is in the form of command and demand: "Give us this day our daily bread, and forgive us our debts as we forgive our debtors," and ends in praise: "For thine is the Kingdom and the Power and the Glory, forever. Amen."

Prayer is command and demand, praises and thanksgiving. The student's work is in making himself believe "with God all things are possible."

Demonstrations often come at the eleventh hour because one then lets go, stops reasoning, and Infinite Intelligence has a chance to work.

I am often asked the difference between *visualizing* and *visioning*. Visualizing is a mental process governed by the reasoning or conscious mind; visioning is a spiritual process governed by intuition, or the superconscious mind. The student should train his mind to receive these flashes of inspiration, and work out the "divine pictures" through definite leads.

When you can say, "I desire only that which God desires for me," your false desires fade from the consciousness, and a new set of blueprints is given to you by the Master Architect, the God within. God's plan transcends the limitation of your reasoning mind, and is always the square of life, containing health, wealth, love, and perfect self-expression.

Turn always to the Christ within. This is your own higher self, made in God's image. This is the self that has never failed, never known sickness or sorrow, was never born, and has never died. It is "the resurrection and the life" within us all.

As you now experience these words, may you be freed from the thing that has held you in bondage, stood between you and your birthright; may you "know the Truth that makes you free"—free to fulfill your destiny, to bring into manifestation the *Divine Design of your life.*

"Be ye transformed by the renewing of your mind."

About the Authors

FLORENCE SCOVEL SHINN was born in Camden, New Jersey, in 1871. She attended the Pennsylvania Academy of Fine Arts, where she met her husband, the realist painter Everett Shinn. She worked for many years as an artist and illustrator of children's literature in New York City before writing her New Thought landmark, *The Game of Life and How to Play It*. Unable to interest New York presses, Shinn published the book herself in 1925. She went on to write three more books: *Your Word is Your Wand,* published in 1928; *The Secret Door to Success*, published in 1940; and *The Power of the Spoken* Word, published posthumously in 1944. Shinn was also a sought-after spiritual lecturer and counselor. She died in New York City in 1940.

MITCH HOROWITZ, who abridged and introduced this volume, is the PEN Award-winning author of books including *Occult America* and *The Miracle Club: How Thoughts Become Reality*. *The Washington Post* says Mitch "treats esoteric ideas and movements with an even-handed intellectual studiousness that is too often lost in today's raised-voice discussions." Follow him @MitchHorowitz.

Printed in the USA
CPSIA information can be obtained
at www.ICGtesting.com
JSHW012046140824
68134JS00034B/3298

9 781722 500535